People Skills for Kids

How to Make Friend & Get Along with Anyone

Caleb Maddix

Table of Contents

Introduction 1

Chapter 1: Showing Interest 5

Chapter 2: Ask Questions 11

Chapter 3: Listening 15

Chapter 4: Let Other People Talk More 19

Chapter 5: Repeating 21

Chapter 6: Eye Contact 25

Chapter 7: Shaking Hands 27

Chapter 8: Be Positive and Enthusiastic 29

Chapter 9: Don't Criticize or Bully 33

Chapter 10: Remember People's Names 35

Chapter 11: Compliment Sincerely 41

Chapter 12: Confidence 43

Chapter 13: Avoid Arguments 45

Chapter 14: Never Assume 47

Chapter 15: Don't Sweat the Small Stuff 49

Chapter 16: Be Open-Minded 51

Chapter 17: Be Quick to Admit You're Wrong ... 55

Chapter 18: See from Other Person's Point of View 57

Chapter 19: Study People...61

Chapter 20: Network..63

Chapter 21: Provide Value...65

Chapter 22: Stand Out...67

Table of Contents

Introduction 1

Chapter 1: Showing Interest 5

Chapter 2: Ask Questions 11

Chapter 3: Listening 15

Chapter 4: Let Other People Talk More 19

Chapter 5: Repeating 21

Chapter 6: Eye Contact 25

Chapter 7: Shaking Hands 27

Chapter 8: Be Positive and Enthusiastic 29

Chapter 9: Don't Criticize or Bully 33

Chapter 10: Remember People's Names 35

Chapter 11: Compliment Sincerely 41

Chapter 12: Confidence 43

Chapter 13: Avoid Arguments 45

Chapter 14: Never Assume 47

Chapter 15: Don't Sweat the Small Stuff 49

Chapter 16: Be Open-Minded 51

Chapter 17: Be Quick to Admit You're Wrong 55

Chapter 18: See from Other Person's Point of View 57

Chapter 19: Study People 61

Chapter 20: Network 63

Chapter 21: Provide Value 65

Chapter 22: Stand Out 67

Introduction

WHHHHHHAAAAAAATTTTTTTTTT'SSS UP, Maddix Addicts! I'm so excited about this book! I wrote, "The Relationship Guide," because it offers a huge list of practical strategies that you can use to strengthen your relationships with anybody and everybody. Listen, guys, I can't stress enough the importance of people skills. If you master this, it will be the key to your success. How do I know this? Because being a master at people skills has given me more opportunities than I could have ever imagined.

There is really no secret to my success. It is a combination of extreme focus and unshakeable work ethic. But the most important element to my success is my ability to connect with people. This skill has allowed me to be invited to celebrities' houses, be featured on national television, get interviewed in magazines, speak all over the world, and make a lot of money in the process. Not only that, it has allowed me to meet and spend time with some of the greatest human beings on the planet. Some of these people weren't millionaires or had a huge amount of success by society's standards. They were just great people that I've met along the way that have given me advice, told memorable stories, and impacted my life in a big way.

I get so frustrated when I see kids staring at their phones or sitting alone in a corner while they are out in public. When they are introduced to someone, they awkwardly say a couple of words and then try to get out of the conversation as quickly as possible. Guys, that is how average kids communicate. You should be savage, and savage kids should be the friendliest, most outgoing, talkative kids on the planet. Every person you meet is an opportunity for you to make a meaningfully connection that could change your life. Even better than that, you could have the ability to change someone else's life as well.

There are some topics that we have already covered in the relationship book that I've included in my other books. There is a reason for this. Repetition is the power of learning. The more that you read and study topics that are presented different ways, the greater your understanding will be. Not only that, your mind will naturally start to act from the information because it will be familiar with the concepts. Don't skip over any of the material because you feel like you already know it. Smart people are identified by their willingness to learn. People that are not so smart feel like they know it all, but they don't really know much about anything.

Before we dig deep into this topic, it is important that you understand that becoming a master at people skills does not guarantee that everyone is going to like you. That is unrealistic. You don't need everyone to like you. There will be times that your personality will just not connect with other people's personalities. That is ok. Your goal should not be to get everyone to like you. Your goal is to just be friendly to everyone you meet and seek to make as many positive connections as possible.

Now, I want you to get your journal, pen, and highlighter and get ready to start taking notes. When you are done reading this, read it again. Carry this book with you until these strategies become habits. Trust me, you are going to want to put ALL of these strategies into action. Let's do this!

Chapter 1
Showing Interest

Guys, I'm going to start off by sharing the number one way to master your people skills, which is to show interest in other people. This will help you stand out in a crowd. Dale Carnegie, author of, *How to Win Friends and Influence People*, said, "You can make more friends in two months by becoming genuinely interested in other people than you can in two years by trying to get people interested in you." This is one of my favorite quotes because it is a consistent reminder of the purpose of communication and connection. When you are speaking with other people, your goal should not be to get them interested in you. You should spend most of the time showing interest in what the other person is saying.

Everyone has something that lights them up. Let me give you an example. You may have a friend that gets super excited about video games. Every time you bring up the subject, your friend can't stop talking about it. Instead of changing the subject because it may not interest you, make this your topic of conversation when you talk to this friend. Discovering a person's passion and what lights them up inside allows you to know how to direct your conversations.

Whenever I talk to people, whether they are my friends or strangers, I am always trying to discover what makes them passionate. One of the strategies I use to discover someone's passion is to ask them what their dream job is. The reason that I do this is that most of the time, people's dream jobs are directly connected to their passion. Their dream job reveals what they really enjoy doing. Once they reveal this, I can simply listen and ask questions, so I can get more information about their dream job.

Showing genuine interest must go beyond simply discovering what lights them up inside. You then must engage them in conversation. There is a difference between talking and actually engaging. When you are engaging with someone, you are not playing on your phone, looking around, or appearing bored. Genuine interest is shown through eye contact, positive body language, and asking questions related to their passion.

I remember when one of my friends bought his first guitar. He loved music and was so excited to learn how to play. When I saw him, he ran up and showed it to me. I could tell that this was super important to him. At that moment, music and his new guitar were his passion. I became as excited as he was. I didn't do this because I'm necessarily passionate about music or playing the guitar. I did this because I genuinely became excited because of the

Chapter 1
Showing Interest

Guys, I'm going to start off by sharing the number one way to master your people skills, which is to show interest in other people. This will help you stand out in a crowd. Dale Carnegie, author of, *How to Win Friends and Influence People*, said, "You can make more friends in two months by becoming genuinely interested in other people than you can in two years by trying to get people interested in you." This is one of my favorite quotes because it is a consistent reminder of the purpose of communication and connection. When you are speaking with other people, your goal should not be to get them interested in you. You should spend most of the time showing interest in what the other person is saying.

Everyone has something that lights them up. Let me give you an example. You may have a friend that gets super excited about video games. Every time you bring up the subject, your friend can't stop talking about it. Instead of changing the subject because it may not interest you, make this your topic of conversation when you talk to this friend. Discovering a person's passion and what lights them up inside allows you to know how to direct your conversations.

Whenever I talk to people, whether they are my friends or strangers, I am always trying to discover what makes them passionate. One of the strategies I use to discover someone's passion is to ask them what their dream job is. The reason that I do this is that most of the time, people's dream jobs are directly connected to their passion. Their dream job reveals what they really enjoy doing. Once they reveal this, I can simply listen and ask questions, so I can get more information about their dream job.

Showing genuine interest must go beyond simply discovering what lights them up inside. You then must engage them in conversation. There is a difference between talking and actually engaging. When you are engaging with someone, you are not playing on your phone, looking around, or appearing bored. Genuine interest is shown through eye contact, positive body language, and asking questions related to their passion.

I remember when one of my friends bought his first guitar. He loved music and was so excited to learn how to play. When I saw him, he ran up and showed it to me. I could tell that this was super important to him. At that moment, music and his new guitar were his passion. I became as excited as he was. I didn't do this because I'm necessarily passionate about music or playing the guitar. I did this because I genuinely became excited because of the joy he received from his first guitar. From that point forward, I would always ask him about his music whenever I would see him. I could tell that he appreciated it and enjoyed communicating with me because I cared about what he cared about.

Now, let's say that my friend came up to show me his guitar and I immediately started talking about something I just bought as well. Would my friend feel like I really cared about his excitement? The truth is that most of us don't enjoy speaking with people who always make the conversation about themselves. You know these types of people. It doesn't matter what you try to talk about, they always point the conversation back to themselves. Conversations with these types of people are usually really unenjoyable. They seem selfish. Remember what Dale Carnegie said. Making friends is more about showing interest in them as opposed to trying to get them interested in you.

While I'm in public, I try to be observant of others. I try to be a study of people, which means I pay attention to what people are wearing, saying, and doing. This helps me communicate more effectively. Let me give you an example. If I'm just meeting someone and they are wearing clothing or a hat with a sports logo on it, I will use that as a conversation opener. I may say, "Oh, you are an Ohio

State fan? That's a shame. You know that's the worst team ever, right?" I use this as a light-hearted joke to get the other person to feel more relaxed, and I also use something that they obviously like so I can connect with them. Most people wear sports logos of teams that they like. This simple conversation starter can allow the person to feel more relaxed and comfortable because I took the time to show interest in something connected them.

If my book, *The Relationship Guide*, I talked about how you should not be selfish in your friendships. This is true for all of your relationships. When you show interest in other people's lives, try to find out as much information as you can about them, and use it to show them that you really care. For instance, in your phone you have a calendar that you can store important dates and events. Start putting all the important birthdates, anniversaries, graduations, etc. of the people that you meet or the other important relationships in your life. When those dates come around, send them a message, buy them a gift, take them out to dinner, etc. You can get creative with this. The point is that when you acknowledge other people's important dates, it shows that you are really interested in what is important to them.

Like I said, asking questions is a quick way to discover the interests of other people. I'm going to give you a few that you can use. As you get better with this, you will start creating your own.

1. What is your dream job?
2. What do you like to do in your spare time?
3. Where would you like to go on vacation?
4. Who is your favorite sports team?
5. What are the top 5 movies/songs/video games?

The most important thing to remember is never try to impress, but always try to show interest. Be quick to listen and slow to speak. When you do speak, let it be about the topic that interests the other person. Pretend you are interviewing someone. The job of an interviewer is not to highlight themselves. Their job is to discover as much as they can about the person they are interviewing. Because of this, they ask questions, listen, and give positive feedback. You will gain more as the interviewer than the one being interviewed.

Chapter 2
Ask Questions

If you become a master at asking questions, you will get the information that some people only dream about getting. When someone is arrested as a suspect in a crime, they go into what is called an interrogation room. In this room, a couple of detectives sit across from the table from the suspect and simply ask them questions. For hours, the detectives come up with questions that will give them the answers that will lead them to the truth. These detectives have spent years studying the kinds of questions they need to ask and the right way to ask them. Their questions are very important because they can determine whether an innocent person goes to prison or guilty person goes free. That's how powerful a question can be.

There is a purpose for asking questions. It is to keep a conversation going. I want to stop right here and make sure that you understand that you are not just asking random questions. That defeats the purpose. Each question should have a specific purpose. A conversation should feel like playing a game of tennis. Asking a question is like serving the ball. The other person answers your question and hits the ball back to you. Once you get the answer, you have to determine how you are going to hit the ball back to them.

In tennis, you don't just swing the racket. You keep your eye on the ball, and when it returns to you, you intentionally hit the ball back to the other side of the court. The same is true with questions. When the answers come back to you, be intentional about how you respond. Are you going to ask another question? Are you going to provide feedback? What type of question are you going to ask next? Stay focused and in the game so you are not just serving a bunch of random questions that don't connect. This will make for a really awkward conversation.

I'm going to provide you with 20 questions that you can ask someone. There are some questions that you can use when you first meet someone. The others are the ones you can use as you get deeper into the conversation. As you get to know people more, you will be able to be more specific with your questions. These are somewhat general, so you can use them for people that you are getting to know. Remember, the key here is to be intentional about the questions that you ask and the way you respond. The more you practice this strategy, the better that you will become.

1. What is your name?
2. What do you want to be when you grow up?
3. Where are you from?

Chapter 2
Ask Questions

If you become a master at asking questions, you will get the information that some people only dream about getting. When someone is arrested as a suspect in a crime, they go into what is called an interrogation room. In this room, a couple of detectives sit across from the table from the suspect and simply ask them questions. For hours, the detectives come up with questions that will give them the answers that will lead them to the truth. These detectives have spent years studying the kinds of questions they need to ask and the right way to ask them. Their questions are very important because they can determine whether an innocent person goes to prison or guilty person goes free. That's how powerful a question can be.

There is a purpose for asking questions. It is to keep a conversation going. I want to stop right here and make sure that you understand that you are not just asking random questions. That defeats the purpose. Each question should have a specific purpose. A conversation should feel like playing a game of tennis. Asking a question is like serving the ball. The other person answers your question and hits the ball back to you. Once you get the answer, you have to determine how you are going to hit the ball back to them.

In tennis, you don't just swing the racket. You keep your eye on the ball, and when it returns to you, you intentionally hit the ball back to the other side of the court. The same is true with questions. When the answers come back to you, be intentional about how you respond. Are you going to ask another question? Are you going to provide feedback? What type of question are you going to ask next? Stay focused and in the game so you are not just serving a bunch of random questions that don't connect. This will make for a really awkward conversation.

I'm going to provide you with 20 questions that you can ask someone. There are some questions that you can use when you first meet someone. The others are the ones you can use as you get deeper into the conversation. As you get to know people more, you will be able to be more specific with your questions. These are somewhat general, so you can use them for people that you are getting to know. Remember, the key here is to be intentional about the questions that you ask and the way you respond. The more you practice this strategy, the better that you will become.

1. What is your name?
2. What do you want to be when you grow up?
3. Where are you from?

4. If you could live anywhere in the world, where would it be? Why?

5. What is your biggest fear?

6. What is your best advice for me?

7. What is something you are obsessed with?

8. Where do you want to go on vacation?

9. What is your favorite thing about school? What is your least favorite?

10. What three words best describe you?

11. If you opened a business, what kind of business would it be?

12. Who in your life brings you the most joy? Why?

13. What's your favorite season? Why?

14. What is something that really annoys you but doesn't bother most people?

15. If you could learn the answer to one question about your future, what would the question be?

16. What do you do to improve your mood when you are in a bad mood?

17. What are you best at?

18. What is the funniest TV series you have ever seen?

19. What book has had the biggest impact on your life?

20. What song always puts you in a good mood?

If you notice, all of these questions are starters to a conversation. They focus on topics that can be discussed for a long period of time. Try to stay away from yes or no questions. These types of questions do not promote a conversation. They lead to a dead end because once they are answered, it can be difficult to figure out what to say next. Open-ended questions start and are able to continue a conversation. A great follow up question is, "Why?" This will cause the other person to go into more detail with their answer.

The 20 questions are merely examples for those of you that need a little more assistance. You do not have to use these exact ones that I've listed. If you have some of your own, use those as well. As you get better with speaking with others, you will be able to ask questions with ease.

Chapter 3
Listening

Have you ever been talking to your parents, and they stop to ask you if you are listening to them? Most of the time, we will answer, "yes," while we role our eyes. Then, they ask you to tell them what they just said to you, and you draw a complete blank. The reason for this is because there is a huge difference between hearing and listening. The difference is that hearing allows you to experience the noise and tones in your ears, but listening involves intentionally focusing on the words spoken, seeking to understand them, and then responding. All these actions must be present in order for listening to really occur. In the example above, I'm sure that you heard your parents. The noise from their mouth was entering your ears. There may even be some words that you remember, but you weren't really listening to them.

Floyd Mayweather is probably one of the greatest boxers of our time. One of the things that makes him so successful is his ability to stay focused and in the moment during his fights. He is watching his opponent's every move and anticipating what he is going to do before he does it. You should be just as in tune and focused when someone is speaking to you. You should be intently listening to what the other person is saying. Be in the moment. Don't be thinking about what you are going to do next or what you are going to eat for dinner. It is usually easy to tell if someone is not listening to you. It can make the conversation be cut short because no one wants to talk to someone that is not listening to them.

There is an older cartoon that features a kid named Charlie Brown. Every time Charlie is in school, the teacher's voice sounds like, "Wah, wah, wah, wah, wah." This would be our modern-day version of, "Blah, blah, blah." Even though the cartoon is funny, it is actually pretty accurate. Most of us start conversations, and when the other person starts talking, we start daydreaming or thinking about something else. You may think that the other person doesn't notice that you are not listening, but most of the time they do. If you are a person that doesn't know how to really listen to other people, then other people will not want to spend time talking with you.

Learning how to listen requires practice and discipline. You have to make a conscious decision to pay attention when someone else is talking. If your mind starts to wander, make yourself refocus. Never get caught going blank in a conversation. When someone asks you a question, never get caught saying, "Huh?" or "What did you say?" These questions show that you really weren't paying attention and can be incredibly frustrating for the person you are talking to.

Don't use the questions from chapter 1 and 2 if you are not going to listen to the answers. That makes the questions pointless. The key is to actively listen to their answers. Even if you are disinterested in the topic, discipline yourself to find something to focus on as they speak. Make sure that all of your distractions have been removed when you are having a conversation. Put your phone away or place it face down on the table. Maintain eye contact with them so your eyes don't start drifting off to other things in the room that may steal your attention.

Imagine you are Floyd Mayweather and all of your conversations are a boxing match. Stay alert and aware of everything that the other person is saying. Don't let them catch you off guard or unfocused. Make sure you walk away from every conversation a winner. If you consistently lose because of your inability to listen, people will make more of an effort to avoid you rather than to try to find an opportunity to speak with you.

CHAPTER 4
Let Other People Talk More

Guys, not only should you listen to other people, you should let them talk more than you do. You should actually be listening more than you talk in any conversation. People love when you listen to them so get them talking and discipline yourself to listen without interrupting and needing to give a lot of feedback. I like to call this method the 80-15-5 method. The way this works is that the rule for conversations is 80% of the time should be spent with the other person talking, 15% should be used for you to ask questions, and 5% is when you can add your feedback.

One thing that I've learned after spending time with successful people, is that they really love to talk, especially if they are sharing advice or wisdom. This is not only true for successful people. Most people love to talk and hear their own voice. It is not because they are prideful, it is just a natural human desire to hear your own voice and share your thoughts with other people. This is the number one key to networking. You don't need to try to sell people on why they need to like you. Doing this actually has the opposite effect. People that are trying to sell themselves or make themselves look important end up looking boring and shallow. However, people that do more listening than talking seem more interesting and make connections easier with other people. Don't try to impress people with your words, intrigue them with your listening ear.

CHAPTER 5
Repeating

I've featured this strategy in previous books, so you must know that if I include information more than once, it is very important. The repeating strategy is so vital for all of your relationships, and it is one of the most helpful tools to increase your listening skills. My dad started having me do this when I was really young, so it's become a habit for me. It is easy for my mind to wander off sometimes, which is why I have disciplined myself to repeat back what I heard the other person say. This holds me accountable to listen to what the person is saying. It also can be used to clarify what they said so there will be no misunderstandings.

Let's do an example. After meeting someone, I may ask them what her dream job is. They may say something like, "My dream job is to own my own clothing line." My response can start with repeating what they just said. "Really, that's awesome that you want to own your own clothing line. How long have you been passionate about clothing?"

You don't have to sound like a robot when you are repeating. You can easily add it into your conversation. We will continue on with the example conversation, so you can really get an idea of the method for repeating. In response to my last question, she states, "When I was a little girl, I used to dress up my dolls and create clothing out of old fabric scraps that my mom had." You could then say, "Wow! That is so cool that your mom had old cloth you could use to dress up your dolls. What kind of outfits would you create?" Once again, I repeated what she said in a unique way, but it still showed that I was actually listening to what she just said.

I also want you to note the way I asked questions. My questions followed along with the conversation and were based on her responses. After she told me what her dream job was, I didn't ask her a totally unrelated question like, "What is your favorite movie?" I stayed with the topic and just built upon it so that we kept a good flow.

Another way you can repeat, is to use their information in a form of a question. I'll give you an example. My dad does this all the time, and it actually works. One time, we were sitting downtown at a coffee shop and my dad started talking to a guy that was sitting at the table next to us. They started talking about sports teams. My dad asked him what his favorite sports team was, and he said the Yankees. My dad responded by saying, "Oh yeah. So, your favorite sports team is the Yankees? Why?" It may sound weird, but rewording people's responses into a question will encourage them to give you more information. Remember, the main purpose of this is to show them that you are listening to what they are saying, and you are interested in more information.

CHAPTER 6
Eye Contact

This strategy is one of the simplest ways to stand out in a crowd. When I see most kids talking with other people, especially adults, they rarely make eye contact. Listen, I totally understand. I used to be like this too. Making eye contact was so uncomfortable for me. It felt weird at first, so I just wouldn't do it. Plus, I was super shy, which meant that making eye contact caused my face to become red and my mind would go blank. It was like being on stage and all of a sudden, the spotlight was shining on my face. To avoid this feeling, I would keep my head down when I talked, or I would look around while the other person was talking.

If you can relate to this, it doesn't mean I'm going to excuse you because I know you can overcome this behavior. How do I know? Because I no longer feel this way about making eye contact. I have mastered this skill and so can you. Even if you feel uncomfortable, you must discipline yourself to do it. Every time you have a conversation, try to maintain eye contact as much as possible. Now, making eye contact does not mean that you stare at them without blinking or looking away. That would be really weird, and the other person might think that there is something wrong with you. Just try to balance out the conversation by making eye contact, then looking away, making eye contact again, and then looking away. Keep this pattern until the conversation is over.

To understand the importance of eye contact, I want you to imagine that you are having a conversation with someone. The whole time you are talking, he is looking at his phone, his eyes keep wandering around the room, and then he stares directly at the floor. I want you to think about how motivated you would be to continue talking with this person. How would you feel during and after the conversation? Would you think that this person was interested in what you were saying? The truth is that people know you are interested and that you care when you are looking them in the eye. It is also a sign of respect.

Mastering this skill will require discipline and practice. Make eye contact even when you don't want to, and do it as much as possible. Find opportunities to have conversations just so you can practice. You can even do this strategy with close friends and family members. Since you are more comfortable, it will be easier to practice on them first. Tell them that you are trying to become better at making eye contact while you are having conversations. Once you are done speaking with them, ask them to give you a grade on how you did with your eye contact.

Chapter 7
Shaking Hands

One morning, my dad and I went to a local the gym. While I was working out, a guy approached me and said, "Man, you are really getting it in. Are you a baseball player?" This was a few years ago when I was pursuing my dream of becoming a professional baseball player. I said, "Yeah, how can you tell?" He told me that it is easy for him to spot a baseball player because he is a scout for professional baseball. We talked for a little bit longer, and he told me that there was something in my eyes that let him know that I was going to be really successful at whatever I did.

Before he left, he shook my hand. As he began to leave, he came back and said, "Whenever you go to shake someone's hand, make sure that it is firm because that shows confidence. Here, let's practice." In the middle of the gym, me and this professional scout were practicing how to shake hands. He wouldn't let me leave until I got it right. From that moment forward, I started shaking everyone's hand the way this guy taught me, and it has made the world of difference.

There is a huge difference between a weak and strong handshake. A person that does a weak handshake, only uses their fingers. The palm of their hand is not involved in the handshake. This type of handshake can communicate fear and insecurity. On the other hand, a firm handshake involves the entire palm and a slight squeeze of the hand. This type of handshake communicates confidence and certainty. Don't squeeze someone's hand so tightly that it becomes painful. You must be aware of the person you are shaking hands with. If it is a lady, still shake with your full hand, but be gentle. If you are a guy shaking another man's hand, you can use a little more force.

Shaking hands might sound simple, but it can actually lead to life-changing opportunities. I went to an event with many powerful and successful people in attendance. One of the people there was Kevin Harrington who is a millionaire, entrepreneur, and was featured on the TV show, "Shark Tank." As I was networking, I introduced myself to him, and he shook my hand. The first thing he said was, "Dude, you have a great handshake." Even though a handshake seems really insignificant, it made me stand out to a powerful business man. After this initial meeting, Kevin Harrington and I became business partners, and it all started with a handshake.

Chapter 8
Be Positive and Enthusiastic

When I was eight, my dad had me listen to and read from a number of motivational speakers, entrepreneurs, and influencers. I grew to respect many of these leaders. One of them was a successful entrepreneur. I read all of his books and listened to his content online. I learned a lot from his material and hoped to one day meet him. A couple of years ago, I attended an event that featured him as a keynote speaker. I was so excited, and I couldn't wait to meet him.

The second day of the event, I sat in the audience during his presentation. About 10 minutes into his talk, he started insulting me over the stage. He said things like, "There's this kid out there who is talking about working your face off. That's not what you need to do. That's ridiculous." He was very negative when speaking about me. I couldn't believe what I was hearing. This guy was not who I thought he was, and he definitely wasn't who he portrayed himself to be in his videos and books.

Now, I could have let this moment really upset me and make me sad. However, it fired me up. I was even more motivated to keep doing what I was doing. Even though he was negative, this incredibly influential entrepreneur and speaker watched my videos and took the time to talk about me over the stage. I wasn't going to let this incident cause me to be ashamed or stop me from trying to connect with other influencers.

After his presentation, I approached him, shook his hand, and asked him if he could do a quick, 10 second SnapChat with me. He glared at me, and said, "No. I don't have time." I then asked if we could get a picture. He seemed annoyed and said no again. After he walked away, I was really disappointed. He was a busy man, I got that. However, his tone, body language, and responses to my questions were negative and rude.

This experience taught me a very valuable lesson. Always be positive and enthusiastic when meeting people because your attitude communicates a lot about your character. It shows that you value and respect other people. Also, don't use your platform or influence to bash other people. It shows how negative you are and could make you appear insecure. I met other people that met this guy as well. All of them had similar experiences. They said that he was negative and an unpleasant person to be around.

Generally, people don't like to be around negative people. It doesn't matter how powerful you are or how much money you have, your impact will be small if you are consistently negative. Positive people have a way of uplifting other people and changing the energy of their environments. Also, negative people usually attract other negative people. I'm sure this guy I talked about had a lot of negative people in his life because he was super negative. Pretty much everyone that is close to me is positive because I am a positive person. Position yourself as someone that is always positive and enthusiastic and other positive people will be attracted to you. Your attitude will make people remember you, and it will set you apart.

Chapter 9
Don't Criticize or Bully

Bullying and criticism are the lowest forms of communication. Only people that are insecure and unhappy with themselves bully and criticize other people. Everyone has been in school with that one guy or girl who is disrespectful to the teacher and bullies another student in the class. People may laugh at bullies and pretend to be friends with them, but the truth is, no one really likes a bully. They may have a place in school, but when they get older, karma starts to do its work. Karma means that what you put out into the world is returned to you. If you criticize and bully other people, the same will end up happening to you.

Never make fun of someone, bully, or gossip about others. Find ways to compliment and celebrate other people. Kindness can positively impact someone's life. Be especially kind to those that are bullied and criticized. They need it more than anyone. Be known for your kindness and compassion. People want to be friends with a kind person. Confident and secure kids don't need to insult other people to make themselves feel good. They find their motivation and fulfillment from lifting other people's spirits through kind words and genuine compliments.

Also, I want to add this. If you are given a compliment, simply accept it. Don't twist them because you feel uncomfortable. For instance, if someone says, "I really like your outfit." Don't say, "Yeah. It's really old and cheap. I've had it forever." This type of response makes it seem like you are insecure. Instead of saying that, simply say, "Thank you." Be humble when you receive compliments, but don't be insecure.

CHAPTER 10
Remember People's Names

Dale Carnegie once said, "Remember that a man's name is to him the sweetest and most important sound in the English language." Think about this for a minute. When you meet someone, the first thing that you do is exchange names. The reason for this is that a person's name identifies them and uniquely separates them from everyone else. Your name is important to you because it is how people remember who you are. Try this exercise. Say the name of someone you know out loud. What do you notice after you say that name? If you are like most humans, saying a person's name that you know makes you start thinking about them. You may get a mental picture of them, think of a memory you have about them, or hear the sound of their voice in your head. That's the power of someone's name.

Remembering peoples' names is important because it shows the other person that you are listening to them and that you value them as an individual. I used to really struggle with remembering people's names. It wasn't because I didn't care about people. I would just easily forget people's names. Since I wanted to be a master of people skills, I knew that I would have to find some practical strategies to help me remember people's names. During my research, I came across a simple acronym that Dale Carnegie created to help people remember names. After I started using this process, I became much better at remembering names. This quickly helped show others that I really valued them by remembering their names.

The acronym that Dale Carnegie created is LIRA.

1. L = Look and Listen

When you first meet someone, make sure that you are focusing on them as they introduce themselves. Sometimes, I can get so caught up in what I'm about to say, that I get distracted. Before I know it, the person told me their name, and I have no idea what it is. Putting this tool into practice helped me to stay in the moment and focus on what the other person was saying.

One thing that I did to keep me focused was once the person said their name, I would imagine it written on their forehead. As they spoke, I maintained eye contact and glanced at their forehead to remind myself of what their name was. There may be an instance when a person shares their name and you are unsure about what they just said. If this happens, simply ask them to repeat it so you can make sure that you know their correct name.

2. I = Impression

After you exchange names, create an impression in your head of the person or situation. You can use the clothes they're wearing or some sort of physical characteristics. For example, if I meet a guy named Bob that is tall, I can associate his name with being tall. I immediately associate Bob with tall.

Another way you can create an impression is using the topics you talked about. Let's say that Bob and I spend time talking about the Yankees. He may love the Yankees. To remember his name, I will connect Bob with the Yankees. Bob = loves Yankees. You can use the environment to remember a name. If I meet Bob at the gym, I'll connect Bob to the gym.

3. R = Repetition

Make it a point to repeat the person's name at least 2 times during the conversation. The key to this is to make it as natural as possible. If you use it before everything that you say, it will sound weird. Let's say that I meet a guy named Sam, and he asks me to give him a strategy to grow his social media. I would respond by saying, "Well, Sam, a strategy to growing your social media is connection. Seek to genuinely connect with your followers before you try to just gain numbers."

Notice that I quickly added his name to the beginning of my response. This does 3 things. 1. Repeating his name helps me remember it. 2. It shows Sam that I was paying attention to him when he introduced himself. 3. It makes Sam feel important because as Dale Carnegie said, a person's name is the sweetest most important sound he could hear. An important note that you must remember is when you are speaking with an adult, use Mr. or Ms. before their name to address them.

When you meet someone new, make it a goal to say their name at least 2 times in the conversation. Once again, don't place their name in awkward points of the conversation. Try to make it sound as natural as possible. As you repeat their name, it will start to stick in your mind, which means that you are more likely to remember it once the conversation is complete. Hours after the conversations, try to repeat the name in your head a few times. It will stick better if you do this.

4. **A = Association**

This one is probably the easiest tool you can use to remember someone's name. Once you hear someone's name, associate it with something else that is familiar to you. For instance, if you meet someone who is named, Danny, and you have an uncle Dan, make that association. You will remember his name easier because he has a similar name to someone that you are already familiar with. You can use movies, songs, books, Bible characters, etc. If someone's name is Harry, you can associate their name with Harry Potter. Making associations can be fun, so get creative as possible.

When you learn this acronym, practice the steps as much as possible. You don't have to use all 4 of them in one conversation, but try to add as many as possible.

Chapter 11
Compliment Sincerely

Compliments can encourage, affirm, and lift someone's spirits. You never know what people are going through, so a genuine compliment can leave a positive lasting impact on someone's life. The key is the word, "genuine." Don't compliment someone if you don't really mean it. For instance, if you tell someone that you like their shoes, make sure that you really like their shoes. Don't just say it because it's the first thing that came into your mind. Everyone has something that you can find to compliment. Be observant and discover something that you like about another person, and be sincere about it. When you pause to really think about your compliments, you can become more creative with what you say, and it will seem more genuine.

I also pay attention to people's accomplishments so that I can support them with genuine compliments. My mom recently wrote a song, and she was really excited about it. When she told me, I made a big deal about it. I complimented her and told her how proud I was. Make this a habit. If someone accomplishes something, be the quickest and the loudest to compliment them.

Chapter 12
Confidence

It was a hot, humid day, and a man decided to go on a walk through the jungle. The first part of his journey was filled with beautiful scenery and soothing sounds of nature. After an hour of walking, the man noticed that he was lost. Without a map or wifi, what was once an enjoyable journey, turned into a panic filled search. All of a sudden, the man noticed a group of lions slowly approaching him. His eyes darted all around him to find a way to escape. He turned in every direction, but the lions quickly surrounded him. His fear became so overwhelming that he curled up into a ball on the ground. He tragically died.

Days later, a group of scientists discovered his body. They soon realized that he was mauled by lions, and one of the scientists slowly shook her head in disappointment. She said, "If only he knew." Another scientist looked at her confused and said, "Knew what?" She said, "Lions are dangerous, but they can sense fear and insecurity. All the man had to do was stand up as tall as he could and raise his hands. Lions respond to confidence differently than fear. Standing with a confident posture would have saved his life, and the lions would not have attacked him."

Lions are a lot like people. We can easily sense insecurity and a lack of authenticity. It can be difficult to have conversations with insecure people that are filled with fear. On the other hand, confident people make conversations more enjoyable. All of the steps we have covered thus far are tools that you can use to help you be a more confident communicator. Be confident when you approach someone to speak. Believe that what you have to say is important and valuable. Think positively about yourself and the other person, and be enthusiastic about what the other person is talking about.

If you are looking for more information on this topic, you can read my book *How to Have Unstoppable Confidence*. I know many of my readers are already putting that information into action and their confidence is building. Remember, repetition is the power of learning, so go over the information covered in my books again and again.

Chapter 13
Avoid Arguments

There is usually no point to arguments, and relationships rarely benefit from them. Most of the time, anger and frustration are the fuel to arguments. Two people end up exchanging harsh words, they start yelling, and the issue does not get resolved. Arguments can really damage relationships because they are filled with negative emotions.

If you get into an argument, it is your fault. It doesn't matter what it was about or who it was with, when you engage in an argument, it is your fault. Why? Because it requires two people. You can't get into one if you refuse to take part in it. Arguments involve a back and forth dialogue between two people. When you remove one of the people, it is no longer an argument. It is the same thing as if you were playing a game. Most games require more than one person, and if you only have one person, you can't play the game.

This means that you have complete power. The only way that you will get into an argument is if you choose to take part in it. You don't have the power to control how other people will respond to you or the way they will treat you, but you do have the power to control how you will respond. You can either completely walk away from the person or change the subject before it escalates. There are some relationships that will not allow you to do this. For example, you can't just walk away from your parents or change the subject. Instead, use a calm tone and don't raise your voice. Hear them out because every time your parents say something, you have an opportunity to learn.

There are times when you will have to participate in uncomfortable conversations, and that is ok. Don't be defensive; rather, learn how to listen to feedback even if it is hard to hear. Arguments usually have some form of truth in them, but most of the time, people don't like to face the truth about themselves, so they become defensive and angry. Choose to avoid arguments at all cost, and seek to have discussions that will help you grow.

Chapter 14
Never Assume

Assuming means to believe that something is true without proof. When you assume something about another person without any proof, you may treat them differently based on false information. Let's say that a new kid comes to school, and your teacher introduces her to the class. All of a sudden, your friend leans over and says, "I heard she is really rude to people." Now, the only information you have about this girl is from your friend who may have heard it from someone else. If you assume this girl is rude without even speaking with her, you may treat her differently because of this. Never assume the worst about anyone even if other people tell you negative information about them. Treat people based on your own experience with them.

If you are going to assume, assume the best and never the worst. Always believe the best, and don't judge others based on how they look or what others say. There have been times that I've heard other kids say they don't like someone else. When I ask them why, they say things like, "She gave me a dirty look," "He seems mean," or "I heard that he said something about me behind my back." There may be times when it does seem like someone doesn't like you or they are treating you poorly. If that is the case, don't assume the worst. Approach them and have a conversation about it. The habit of making assumptions will make you a suspicious person that treats other people poorly just because you think the worst about someone without proof. Don't be that type of kid. Be the kid that looks for the best in everyone and the one that always assumes the best.

Chapter 15
Don't Sweat the Small Stuff

Every Christmas, my dad and I go to a cabin in Tennessee to relax and recharge before the new year. One year, we were sitting in a hot tub at night while we were talking to each other. A 63-year-old security officer walked by, and we started a conversation with him. As I usually do, I asked him a question. I said, "Sir, what is your best advice for me?" He said, "Don't sweat the small stuff because everything is small stuff." This has probably been one of the best pieces of advice I've ever received. There have been times that I've been reminded of this advice in moments when I needed it most.

Working with my dad is probably one of the greatest blessings in my life. However, there are times when it can present some challenges. I remember there was a span of time when it seemed like me and my dad were constantly disagreeing. It was causing frustration, and I couldn't seem to figure out why we weren't getting along.

One of my close friends was working with us at the time, and I asked him to go on a walk with me. As we were walking, I asked him, "What do you think I'm doing wrong? Why do my dad and I keep disagreeing?" He said, "Dude, you are sweating the small stuff. You get so defensive. Just let all that stuff go. If you get upset, let it go quickly." Immediately after he said that, I remembered the advice from the security guard. I had been focusing too much on the small stuff that really didn't matter. When I put my life in perspective and followed that advice, our disagreements immediately decreased.

Rule of 5 – If it's not going to matter in 5 years, then don't spend 5 minutes on.

Life is too short to be focused on stuff that really is not all that important. Pick your battles. Decide what needs to be addressed and discussed, and then let go of everything else. Don't spend so much time getting upset or arguing about things that don't really matter. Have the self-control to let go of the things that may upset you. If it's a life and death issue or it has the potential to impact your future, address it calmly and respectfully. Otherwise, be the type of kid that recognizes the small stuff and quickly gets over it. I like to call this concept the rule of 5. If it's not going to matter in 5 years, then don't spend 5 minutes on it. This will minimize the number of things you think about and stress over.

CHAPTER 16
Be Open-Minded

A close-minded person believes that their perspective and opinion is right and everyone else is wrong. An open-minded person has a perspective and opinion, but they are open to viewing life differently and respecting others that may not be like them.

Open-minded people:

1. Are always willing to learn

They don't just want information that affirms what they already believe. They are researching and listening to things that present different information. If someone presents different information, they don't dismiss them as wrong. Rather, they willingly listen and seek to learn and grow.

2. Take Correction

This is difficult for most people. Everyone wants to hear praise and compliments but few like to hear about areas that need improvement. You will never be able to grow without receiving correction. I used to hate correction. When my dad would tell me something that I needed to improve, I would become upset and defensive. I didn't want to hear anything that I considered negative about myself, even though I knew it was true. The problem with that is I was stunting my growth. If you are unwilling to hear about your weak areas, you will never be able to improve them. Open minded people know that taking correction can be difficult, but they welcome it because they understand it's a key part of their growth.

3. Listen to Other People's Opinions

Open-minded people will never insult someone's opinions no matter how foolish they may seem. Remember, everyone's opinions are deeply personal and connected to their beliefs. Just because someone has a different opinion than you, doesn't mean they are wrong or weird. Celebrate other people's opinions because it is what makes us unique. Listen to other people's opinions. You may learn something new and become better for it.

4. Sometimes the right thing is to be wrong

Sometimes we hold on to our beliefs so tightly that we will defend them no matter what. There is nothing wrong with strong beliefs, but if you are always trying to convince people that you are right, you avoid opinions and conversations that may challenge your beliefs. If someone disagrees with you, that is ok. They are allowed to do that. Don't waste your time and energy trying to convince other people that you are right. Base your life on your beliefs and values without feeling like you need to prove yourself to other people.

5. **Don't get Stuck in Their Ways**

Many times, people make decisions based on the mentality, "This is the way I've always done it." The inability to change can cause people to become very unsuccessful. Years ago, there was a video store called Blockbuster. They used to rent movies to their customers. When movies started to stream online, Blockbuster refused to make any changes to their products. They believed that their method was best despite the market saying otherwise. People were watching movies on their computers and smart phones and no longer wanted to go to a store to rent movies.

Because Blockbuster was unwilling to change their method, they went out of business. The fact that some of you don't even know what Blockbuster is shows how important it is to always be reinventing yourself. Always be open to changing how you do things or how you view the world. The most adaptable people are usually the most successful. Don't get stuck in your ways of thinking and learning. Be open to evolving and changing on a regular basis.

Chapter 17
Be Quick to Admit You're Wrong

Each week, I have to pay close attention to my schedule and make sure nothing overlaps. I also have to be aware of the time I am spending on each task. During one of our Monday morning meetings, my dad told me that I shouldn't schedule anymore events for the rest of the month. Without seeking any more feedback, I immediately disagreed. I told my dad that I wanted to schedule at least 2 more events.

Pulling out the schedule, I showed my dad some of the free dates. Despite my reasoning, my dad still warned me that it would be too much, and I would be in danger of not being able to fulfill all my responsibilities. After that conversation, I was convinced that I was right. It didn't seem like it would be too much to add extra events to my calendar.

Within a week, I received 2 invitations to speak that next month. I was so excited and booked both dates. At our next morning meeting, we were going over our schedule for the next month. My dad saw the new dates on the calendar and looked at me with disappointment. He said, "Caleb, do you realize that you double booked one of these events. You didn't notice that you already had an event already scheduled on the weekend you just booked. Son, that is one the reasons why I told you to avoid filling your calendar."

Even though I was embarrassed about my error, I still didn't want to admit I was wrong. In that moment, my pride started to arise, but instead of getting upset and trying to defend myself, I looked at my dad, apologized, and told him I was wrong. It was hard to do, but it was the right thing to do because I was wrong. I should have listened to my dad's advice. My mistake meant that I was going to have to cancel one of the events, which was upsetting. I realized that it's always better to be wrong way before the wrong hurts. The schedule was too packed, and I shouldn't have scheduled anything else. I was trying to prove that I wasn't wrong, and I ended up causing issues for myself and my business.

After I quickly admitted my error, my dad told me that he forgave me, and he respected me for admitting that I was wrong. Guys, it's never easy to admit that you are wrong, but people will respect you more if you are able to do so. Admitting you're wrong will save you from unnecessary arguments and keep you from being too prideful. If you are wrong, own up to it and apologize. This gives you the opportunity to make it right and not get the reputation of being a know it all that can't admit when they are wrong.

Chapter 18
See from Other Person's Point of View

Every person on the planet is unique. We all have different personalities, experiences, and perspectives. That's what makes life so interesting, and it is what makes people skills necessary. Our differences are what fuels our conversations. This may sound like common knowledge, but it is something that we easily forget. We actually believe that everyone thinks like us, acts like us, and has the same opinions as us. That is absolutely not true.

There will be times that you may upset someone or disagree with them. Most of the time, we try to get the other person to see our perspective. We put a lot of effort into trying to make them understand us, but we spend little time trying to understand the other person. Being able to see life from another person's perspective is a people skill that many people do not possess, even adults. It can be difficult to look past how people present themselves to see who they really are.

Let me give you an example. Let's say that you get into a fight with your mom after school. She tells you to clean up your room, and you tell her that you will do it in a little bit. All of a sudden, your mom becomes super angry and starts yelling at you. Her response makes you become defensive and you start arguing with her. As we discussed earlier, this only results in both of you being upset and you being punished and sent to your room. After you have some time to cool off, you start to really think about what made your mom upset. You try to look at life from your mom's perspective.

She works long hours, cleans the house, prepares dinner, always makes sure that everyone is ok, and doesn't get much sleep. Maybe her yelling wasn't just about your messy room. Maybe your mom was frustrated and tired. Maybe she had a long day. Maybe she was already upset about something else and your disobedience triggered an emotional reaction. Then, you try to put yourself in her shoes. You ask yourself, "What if that was me? How would I respond in that moment?" You can use this same exercise with any of your family members, friends, or even new acquaintances. Try to put yourself in their shoes and see life from their perspective.

When you try to see life from someone else's perspective, it allows you to become more empathetic and compassionate. You realize that everyone is not like you. Their responses and reactions go deeper than what we may be able to see in the moment. If you take some time to figure out how another person is really feeling or who they really are, it will help you communicate better with them and show them the love that they may need. It will become easier to apologize and treat others kindly when you realize that people can go through a great deal of difficulty without anyone really knowing.

Chapter 19
Study People

Anytime I'm in public, I do this thing called people watching. I know it may sound creepy, but it's actually a great strategy to use for learning more about people. It is interesting to watch the different ways people interact with each other. I've watched some people talk to one another as they sit close and maintain eye contact. I've also seen people sit across from each other and look at their phones the whole time. Because I want to understand more about the way people communicate and relate to one another, I'm always watching and observing.

Doing this helped me become a better communicator. I began to relate to people better, and my relationships improved. The main person that I started to observe was my dad. He is probably one of the greatest masters of people skills that I know. He would talk to people all the time, listen to them, and ask questions. I watched his body language and listened to his tone of voice. I also noticed the types of questions that he asked and how he responded to questions. I began to mimic some of the behaviors I saw because I wanted to become a master of people skills as well. I encourage you to do the same. Find someone that you admire who has great people skills. Watch the way they relate to other people and start mimicking their behaviors.

You can also study people while you are having a conversation. Watch the body language of the other person and notice their tone of voice. Pay attention to their energy and overall mood. Once you discover these things, try to mimic it. For example, if you start talking with someone and they are speaking in a low tone of voice, lower your voice as well. If you are talking with someone that has a lot of energy, start responding with that same amount of energy. People like people that are like them, so modeling the same behavior will make them feel more safe and comfortable with you.

CHAPTER 20
Network

Networking simply means to connect with groups of people or individuals. The purpose of networking is to be known by a lot of people. The more people you know, the more opportunities you have to form life-changing and beneficial relationships that will impact your future. When I used to play baseball, I would talk to every umpire and coach that I could find at all of our tournaments. I knew that if I wanted to go pro, I would need the attention of as many people as possible. Networking with umpires and coaches allowed me to receive advice and feedback that I needed to become a better player. Also, the fact that I intentionally spoke with them, made them remember my name.

Now that I'm pursuing entrepreneurship, I'm using the same method. I'm trying to meet as many people as I can because a huge part of success is determined by who you know and not always what you know. Once I make a connection, I try to keep it by staying in touch. I want you to look over the goals you have. Who do you need to know that will help you achieve those goals? For example, if you want to be an author, who do you need to know that will help you achieve that goal? You may need to meet someone that owns a publishing company or someone that is already a published author.

If I were still a baseball player, I would be posting videos of my games and practices to all my social media pages. I would then share it with as many players, scouts, agents, and sports pages that I could find. I would do this because I understand that I will have a greater chance of meeting people that can actually help me achieve my goal.

Chapter 21
Provide Value

Mastering this skill will set you apart from everyone else because it is one of the most neglected skills. Sometimes we can be so selfish that we are always trying to figure out how we can get other people to do things for us. This is true even when it comes to relationships. We are always seeking to receive from other people before we seek to give. Savage kids are different. I want you to make it a point to figure out how you can provide value to every single person you meet. Providing value doesn't always mean that you have to physically give something. You could give an encouraging word, a compliment, advice, or information on something that would help them.

I've talked about providing value to your mentors in other books, but I want you to remember the importance of doing this. Don't be selfish when it comes to your relationship with your mentors. Seek to provide value to them as much as they are providing it to you. One of my mentors is one of the top marketers in the world. He has made millions of dollars at a young age, and I've learned so much from him. During one of his keynote speeches, he mentioned from stage that he wanted to become better at social media. After the event, I approached him and offered him my social media course for free. The course gives valuable information that I've discovered and used to create viral videos and connect with more people online. In exchange for that, he helped me market some of my products and services for my business. This is an example of the law of exchange. When you seek to add value to others first, you will receive value in return. It might not always be from the same person, but you will receive it in return.

Chapter 22
Stand Out

I waited until the end to add this one because I think it sums up all the strategies I've included in this book. The best way to become a master at people skills is to simply stand out. Everything that we discussed in this book is to help you become savage and refuse average. For the rest of your life, I want you to stay away from average like you would a deadly disease.

Don't settle for becoming like every other kid your age that can't even have a full conversation with an adult. Don't stand in the corner in a crowded room looking at your phone. Don't just talk to the people that are in your circle of friends or family. Challenge yourself to stand out from everyone else. Be ok with being different and extreme. If you practice these strategies and make them a habit, you will be one of the most memorable, successful kids on the planet. People will remember your name, and when they hear it, a smile will spread across their face. Now, Maddix Addicts, it's time to go out there and change the world.

CPSIA information can be obtained
at www.ICGtesting.com
Printed in the USA
LVHW012246221219
641424LV00017B/1553